YOUNG PEOPLE IN RECOVERY

STEP 2

for young adults

Jane Nakken, C.C.D.P.

About the booklet: This booklet is intended to be used as a guide for young adults taking their Second Step toward recovery. It provides space for written responses to questions designed to lead the reader toward awareness and acceptance of a chemical dependency problem.

About the author: Jane Nakken is a chemical dependency counselor and is manager of treatment services at Hazelden Pioneer House, a treatment center for young adults. She is author of **Enabling Change** and **Straight Back Home**, and coauthor of **Step One For Young Adults**, all published by Hazelden Educational Materials.

STEP 2
FOR YOUNG ADULTS

Jane Nakken

HAZELDEN

First published January, 1986.

ISBN 13: 978-1-089486-351-6

Printed in the United States of America.

INTRODUCTION

Hope for Recovery

You have come to understand you are a chemically dependent person. For most of us, this is a time that is both wonderful and terrible.

It is terrible because we have looked hard at the pain inside and at the mess our lives are in; we feel sad, sick and sorry about what has happened to us. We may feel guilty for the trouble our behavior has caused others. We also know we have more thinking to do about our pain and our healing.

But it is also wonderful, because now we know *why* it has happened — because we have a disease more powerful than we are. It's not our fault. How often have we told people that before, when we were using? But now it's not just an excuse that feels strangely true — we have admitted and started to accept that it *is* the truth.

But if our chemical dependency is more powerful than we are, how can we possibly stay sober? We have admitted we can't control our chemical use or its effects on our lives, so how are we supposed to recover?

The answer suggested by A.A. is simple: find someone or something that can help you. Everyone who has a serious disease needs help — even doctors go to other doctors. There is help available for us, just as there is help for people with other diseases. We are responsible for finding the best help available to help us recover from our chemical dependency.

Step Two is: **Came to believe that a Power greater than ourselves could restore us to sanity.**

1

CHAPTER ONE

Why do we need Step Two?

Because in taking Step One, we realize we have a very scary disease that has had control over us. We know we are in trouble and need help. Everyone needs help to recover from diseases, and we do, too. But regular doctors can't cure us because our disease is a disease of the mind, body, and spirit. We need a special kind of help.

Step Two asks us to think about where we can get the help we need. We each make our own choice, based on who we are and what we believe, but A.A. suggests we make a choice of *something* to go to for help. This pamphlet is a tool to use in thinking about finding a Higher Power you can believe in. One that can help you recover from your chemical dependency.

Our first reactions

Most of us took one look at Step Two and said something like, "I knew this must be the wrong program for me, and this proves it. It's a program for crazy people. I don't need to be restored to sanity — I'm not insane!"

Then we thought about Step One some more and decided, "Well, maybe I'm just a little insane — but only when I'm using chemicals!" Then we remembered we haven't been able to stop using and stay stopped. Some of us looked up **sanity** and found meanings like *soundness of mind* or *soundness of judgment* or *healthy balance.* We looked over the examples we wrote down when we were working on our First Step, and they proved to us we could use some sanity in our lives.

What about *soundness of mind?* All of us have had times when our minds weren't working right. Just being high, for example. But many of us have had other proof our minds weren't working normally because of chemicals, such as blackouts, hallucinations, and loss of memory.

Blackouts are not normal. A blackout is loss of memory about what we were doing for a period of time. We don't remember blackouts. We usually figure out we had them because things don't add up to us — like, we were in one place and then we were somewhere else, but we don't remember how we got there. Or a friend starts talking about what happened at a party as if we should know what they are talking about because we were there, but we don't.

Our minds are not working normally when we have **hallucinations.** A hallucination is when we see or hear or feel something that is not there, or we see or hear it differently than it really is. We can have hallucinations when we are high or when we are sobering up.

One last test of soundness of mind is how well we are able to remember and to learn new things. Most of us found we seemed to forget more often and had trouble on the job or in our schoolwork when we had to think in order to do it.

Think about how these problems applied to you when you were using. Write three examples of how your mind was *unsound* when you were using. Your examples might be things that happened to you because of **blackouts, hallucinations,** or **poor memory.**

1.

2.

3.

How about *soundness of judgment?* **Sanity** means having sound judgment. We were certainly missing that while we were using! We found our chemicals making our choices for us, and many of them were poor ones. We did many things we can look back on now and see were dangerous, hurtful, or just plain dumb. Because of our bad judgment, we may have lost good friends, dropped out of activities we liked, started failing in school, and even put our lives or the lives of others in danger. List a few of the things you did as a result of your chemical dependency that show you didn't have *sound judgment:*

    1.

    2.

    3.

    4.

The last meaning for **sanity** is *healthy balance.* It means living in a way that is good for us and helps us grow as well-rounded people. Chemically dependent people who are still using aren't in healthy balance. One thing — our high — takes more of our time, energy, money, and love than anything else in our life. We lose other interests, goals, and relationships.

What are some ways your life got out of balance because of your using?

1.

2.

3.

4.

5.

So, after thinking about it, we can see pretty clearly we were not sane while we were using. If you have gotten this far in this pamphlet, you are probably able to see that, too.

But the amazing thing to realize is we did the **most** insane thing over and over, and we did it sober. We took that first drink, or joint, pill, line, sniff, snort, etcetera — knowing (and denying) it meant trouble. We couldn't control our use of chemicals, no matter how many times we tried. Some of us gave up trying. We could not restore ourselves to sanity. But, for each of us, something happened that changed the hopeless craziness and helped us to begin recovering — we **Came to believe that a Power greater than ourselves could restore us to sanity.**

CHAPTER TWO

Came to believe. . .

Step Two starts out by letting us know that it will take a while to understand it. It says, "Came to believe," **not** "All of a sudden I knew," or, "finally decided that the preacher was right," or, "a thunderbolt hit me and then I believed." It says, "Came to believe." Coming to believe takes what it takes, and we can't **make** it happen. We can **help** it happen, though. We can do this by thinking about it, remembering how it was when we used to have faith in something, and recalling where we get our help and support.

Some of us get turned off when we read Step Two because it sounds like God stuff. We're afraid the A.A. program is going to say we have to believe in God. And we don't believe in God. Or we believe there is a God but we don't think this God has much to do with our lives. Or we believe in God, but don't trust Him or Her. Or we are afraid we're in trouble with God because we haven't been perfect.

Perhaps we have other spiritual beliefs or no beliefs at all, and we don't want to be brainwashed.

Relax. You don't have to believe in God. Or Buddha or Yin and Yang. Step Two simply suggests we find something to believe in that can help us recover.

Spirituality

The program of recovery suggested in A.A. is called a **spiritual** program. Spirituality is not the same thing as religion. **Spiritual** means it has to do with our spirit.

We each have our own spirit. Our spirit is the invisible part of us that gives us life and energy. When people are depressed, we say their spirits are low. When a person has died, we say his or her spirit has gone. When we are really happy, we say we are in *high* spirits. Isn't that one reason we used chemicals — to get that *high* we hoped would make us happy? Our spirit makes us all a little bit different from each other and special in our own way. Our feelings, beliefs, moods — everything that makes a personality — comes from the spirit.

What are some parts of your spirit that you already know pretty well?

What is your favorite color?

What is your favorite song?

Who do you look up to the most?

What is your favorite season of the year?

What is your favorite place?

Do you have a good sense of humor?

Are you a serious person?

Are you quiet or do you talk a lot?

How do you feel inside most of the time?

Who are your best friends?

1.

2.

3.

What makes you sad?

1.

2.

3.

What makes you happy?

1.

2.

3.

Spirituality is the way we help our spirits be alive and happy. We all have spiritual things we do. Some work, some don't. We may have used alcohol or other drugs to make our spirits feel better. Instead, our spirits got sick and tired.

What are some other spiritual things you do?

Have you ever been to a place that made your spirit feel joy, peace, or awe? Where was that?

1.

2.

3.

What special people in your life bring good feelings when you are with them or think about them?

1.

2.

3.

What special things do you do alone or with other people to make your spirit feel alive and happy?

1.

2.

3.

4.

5.

When we say the Twelve Step program is a **spiritual** program, we mean it helps us learn some new ways to take very good care of our spirit. Step Two asks us to begin by coming to believe in a Higher Power that can heal our spirit.

CHAPTER THREE

Finding our own Higher Power

How can we choose a Power greater than ourselves that can restore us to sanity? The same way we would choose someone to help us with any serious problem. We want someone who knows what needs to be done and how to do it, is strong enough to do it, and cares about us enough to put a lot of work into us. Let's look at these one at a time.

You will probably want a Higher Power who knows all about chemical dependency and recovery, and as much as possible about you. This is what we mean by a power that is *higher* — when it comes to what we need, we are going to the expert.

List some persons or things that know about chemical dependency, recovery, and you:

1.

2.

3.

4.

5.

6.

7.

8.

When we need other kinds of expert help, we ask for recommendations from people who have gotten good help. That is a good idea now, before you choose a Higher Power for your recovery program. Ask some recovering people who seem to be getting healthy what they believe in as a Higher Power and how it works for them. List their answers.

1.

2.

3.

4.

5.

We also need a Higher Power that is not only smart, but *powerful.* It can restore us to sanity. You have already asked others how their Higher Power works for them, so you have probably been thinking about how a Higher Power could work for you.

List the Higher Powers you think might work, and write a little bit about **how** that Higher Power could help you recover.

1.

2.

3.

Once you've found a Higher Power you believe is expert enough and strong enough to restore you to sanity, there's really only one big question left — **will it care enough** to restore you to sanity? Can you trust it to be there when you need help? Will it give up on you or hang in there when the going gets rough?

Most of us need a Higher Power that doesn't expect us to be perfect. It helps if our Higher Power is not only caring, but also has a good sense of humor, and lots of understanding and forgiveness. Can you choose a Higher Power you believe could restore you to sanity? Write a little bit about the Higher Power you have chosen:

A final thought

. . . restore us to sanity means to return us to the sanity we used to have. Most of us were more or less sane before our chemical dependency took over our lives. However, we were quite a bit younger than we are now. We know we don't gain much maturity when we are spending our lives chasing a high, and walking around intoxicated much of the time.

You will be taking a better look at yourself when you get to Step Four, so you can get your bearings as you begin recovery. But for now, just remember you have some catching up to do to make up for the growing you lost in the years your disease had control. That's normal. Go easy; ask for what you need to help you. Remember, being restored to your former sanity is a good start, and you will be able to catch up mentally, emotionally, and spiritually as you work your Twelve Step program.

This booklet is one person's interpretation of part of Alcoholics Anonymous' Twelve Step program. The Twelve Steps to recovery are as follows:

1. We admitted we were powerless over alcohol — that our lives had become unmanageable.
2. Came to believe that a Power greater than ourselves could restore us to sanity.
3. Made a decision to turn our will and our lives over to the care of God *as we understood Him.*
4. Made a searching and fearless moral inventory of ourselves.
5. Admitted to God, to ourselves, and to another human being the exact nature of our wrongs.
6. Were entirely ready to have God remove all these defects of character.
7. Humbly asked Him to remove our shortcomings.
8. Made a list of all persons we had harmed, and became willing to make amends to them all.
9. Made direct amends to such people wherever possible, except when to do so would injure them or others.
10. Continued to take personal inventory and when we were wrong promptly admitted it.
11. Sought through prayer and meditation to improve our conscious contact with God *as we understood Him,* praying only for knowledge of His will for us and the power to carry that out.
12. Having had a spiritual awakening as the result of these Steps, we tried to carry this message to alcoholics, and to practice these principles in all our affairs. *

---

* The Twelve Steps reprinted with permission of A.A. World Services, Inc.

Other titles that will interest you . . .

Hazelden Step Pamphlets for Young Adults

This series of large-format pamphlets is written specifically to help young adults work the Twelve Steps of Alcoholics Anonymous. Each pamphlet uses a simple, straightforward workbook format that carries them through a comprehensive self-examination to discover a useful and practical understanding of the Twelve Steps.

Step One for Young Adults
by Jane Nakken, C.C.D.P., and Della Van Dyke, C.C.D.P.
Order No. 1362

Step Three for Young Adults
by Della Van Dyke, C.C.D.P.
Order No. 5502

Step Four for Young Adults
(formerly *An Adventure in Self-Discovery*)
by Paul Bjorklund
Order No. 1129

Step Five for Young Adults
by Lawrence L. Hyde
Order No. 5505

Young Adult Pamphlet Collection, Steps One through Five
Order No. 0828

Keep It Simple

Daily meditations in clear, contemporary language concentrate on the fundamentals of Twelve Step recovery from chemical dependency. *Keep It Simple* helps young adults take responsibility for their sobriety, and lends the support and encouragement necessary to work a successful program. Suggested activities help put key recovery concepts to work. 400 pp.
Order No. 5066

Young, Sober & Free, Second Edition
by Shelly Marshall

Written by and for young persons, this book tells the story of alcoholism and other drug addiction and how many young men and women have found the way to sobriety and freedom.
Order No. 2016

Feed Your Head

Some Excellent Stuff on Being Yourself
written by Earl Hipp, illustrated by L.K. Hanson

Drawing on their own experiences, comments from scores of young people, and healthy doses of humor, the author and illustrator of this eclectic guide offer off-the-wall advice to survive and thrive the stress of teen life. From the "human volcano" to "chicken courage," teen readers will find help in deciding how they can be the best person possible. 150 pp.
Order No. 5034

For price and order information, or a free catalog, please call our Telephone Representatives.

HAZELDEN

Pleasant Valley Road
P.O. Box 176
Center City, MN 55012-0176

1-800-328-9000 (Toll Free. U.S., Canada, Virgin Islands)
1-651-213-4000 (Outside the U.S. & Canada)
1-651-213-4590 24-hour (FAX)
http://www.hazelden.org

ISBN 978-0-89486-351-6

9 780894 863516

Order No. 5501